MW01053894

This notebook is intended to be used as part of the ARTES LATINAE program.

ARTES LATINAE LEVEL ONE
REFERENCE NOTEBOOK

by Waldo E. Sweet and John Arbogast

BOLCHAZY-CARDUCCI PUBLISHERS

1000 Brown Street, Wauconda, Illinois 60084

Formerly published by Encyclopaedia Britannica Educational Corporation

Copyright © 1983 Bolchazy-Carducci Publishers, Inc.

Previous Copyright © 1966 by Encyclopaedia Britannica
Educational Corporation.

All rights reserved. This work may not be transmitted by
television or other devices or processed nor copied, recast,
transformed, adapted or utilized in any manner, in whole or in
part, without a license. For information regarding license,
write:

Bolchazy-Carducci Publishers, Inc.
1000 Brown Street, Unit 101
Wauconda, IL 60084
http://www.bolchazy.com

PRINTED IN THE UNITED STATES OF AMERICA
by United Graphics

1999 REPRINT

ISBN 0-86516-295-6

TABLE OF CONTENTS

TO THE STUDENT

Latin: Level One is so designed that, if you follow directions, you will learn almost all the material perfectly. However, there may well come a time when you would like to see a brief summary of the material you have covered. This is the purpose of this Reference Notebook, which you will construct as you progress through the programmed materials.

One of the things you will learn in this course is to be accurate. Nowhere will the need for accuracy be more apparent to you than in this Notebook, for you will be able to study profitably from it only if you have copied the information accurately.

FACTS ABOUT LATIN

1. A _____ _____ in Latin is marked by a _____ over the

   vowel. (Unit 3, #52)

2. The contrast in form between _____ and _____ and between

   _____ and _____ is the chief difference between

   _____ and _____ . (Unit 4, #113)

3a. Latin *never* signals _____ or _____ by

   _____ but by the signals { ___ } and { ___ }. (Unit 4, #137)

3b. In Latin, word order is _____ _____ _____ .
   (Unit 6, #98)

4. While _____ ? asks for the { ___ } of the sentence, _____ ? asks for the

   { ___ } of the sentence. (Unit 7, #31)

5. The _____ case of a _____ noun or adjective is

   always like the _____ case; there are ___ exceptions

   to this rule. (Unit 16, #33)

6. _____ nouns always end in - ___ in the _____ .

   _____ _____ ; there are ___ exceptions to

   this rule. (Unit 16, #34)

7. _____ in Latin are always _____ before - ___ and always

   _____ before - ___ . (Unit 16, #161)

8. _____ asks for a _____ noun.

   _____ asks for a _____ noun.

   _____ _____ asks for ___ _____ .

   _____ _____ asks for a _____ of the _____ .
   (Unit 16, #371)

3

9. Because of its _____, the ____ ____ _____ sentence is

one of the _____ _____ structures in Latin.
(Unit 17, #30)

10. The prepositions ____, ___, _____, _____, __ (and ____),

_____, and _____ pattern with the _____ case.
(Unit 19, #388)

11. The _____ case is used with adjectives like _____

(Unit 20, #48) and _____ (Unit 21, #70).

12. The _____ _____ in Latin is expressed by the

_____ case. (Unit 20, #180)

13. The _____ case is used as the _____ of the special

verbs _____, _____, _____, _____,

and _____ . (Unit 21, #278)

14. The _____ case is used with compound verbs like _____

(Unit 21, #291) and _____ (Unit 22, #129).

15. In *Latin: Level One*, the only use of the _____ case is to have one

noun _____ another. (Unit 22, #33)

16. The #___ form of the verb describes an action which was _____

_____ in the past. Possible English translations of **cēnābat**

are " ____ _____ ____ _____," " ____ _____

(_____)," " ____ _____ ____ _____,"

" ____ _____ ____ _____," " ____ _____ ____ ____

_____ ____ _____," etc. (Unit 26, #79)

17. The #___ form of the verb describes an action which is not completed at the

_____ time. Possible English translations of **cēnat** are " ____ ____

_____ (_____ _____)," and " ____ _____

(_____)." (Unit 26, #80)

4

18. The #___ tense shows _____ action in _____ time.

Plōrābimus may be translated in English by "____ _____ _____

____ _____," " ____ _____ _____," and in several other ways.
(Unit 26, #241)

19. The #___ tense may describe an action which is _____ complete at the

_____ time. In the right context, Mūrēs cēpit could mean,

" ____ _____ _____ _____ _____ (_____

_____ _____ _____ ___ _____

_____)." (Unit 27, #161)

20. A second common use of the #___ tense is to describe an action which happened

in _____ time as in _____ __ _____ . In the right con-

text, Mūrēs cēpit could mean, " ____ _____ _____ _____."

Perhaps he _____ _____ them; perhaps he _____ _____ ____

_____ . (Unit 27, #162)

5

LATIN FORMS

Fill in these forms as soon as you meet them in your text.

NOUNS

I.

Nominative	virØ	manuS	mūsØ	vestiS
Accusative				
	(Unit 5, #128)	(Unit 5, #129)	(Unit 5, #130)	(Unit 5, #131)
Nominative	datorØ	vēritāS	diēS	DeuS
Accusative				
	(Unit 5, #132)	(Unit 5, #133)	(Unit 5, #134)	(Unit 5, #135)

II.

	First___ Declension	_____ Declension	
Nominative	fēmin	agn	vir
Accusative			
Ablative			
	(Unit 9, #374)	(Unit 9, #375)	(Unit 9, #376)

	_____ Declension	_____ Declension	
Nom	fūr	pisc	mors
Acc			
Abl			
	(Unit 9, #377)	(Unit 9, #378)	(Unit 10, #430)

_____ Declension

Nom	**di**_____
Acc	_____
Abl	_____

(Unit 10, #431)

III. NEUTER NOUNS

	Second Declension	Third Declension
Nom	**vitium**	**opus**
Acc	___ ____	_____
Abl	_____	_____

(Unit 12, #466) (Unit 12, #467)

IV.

	Singular	Plural
Nom	**sīmia**	_____ (1)
Acc	_____	_____
Abl	_____	_____

(Unit 15, #109)

	Singular	Plural	Singular	Plural
Nom	**lupus**	_____ (2)	**vir**	_____ (2)
Acc	_____	_____	_____	_____
Abl	_____	_____	_____	_____

(Unit 15, #110) (Unit 15, #111)

	Singular	Plural		Singular	Plural
Nom	**canis**	_____ (3)	Nom	**leō**	_____ (3)
Acc	_____	_____	Acc	_____	_____
Abl	_____	_____	Abl	_____	_____

(Unit 15, #112)   (Unit 15, #113)

	Singular	Plural
Nom	**manus**	_____ (4)
Acc	_____	_____
Abl	_____	_____

(Unit 15, #114)

	Singular	Plural
Nom	**rēs**	_____ (5)
Acc	_____	_____
Abl	_____	_____

(Unit 15, #115)

V. NEUTER NOUNS

Second Declension

	Singular	Plural
Nom	**rēgnum**	_____
Acc	_____	_____
Abl	_____	_____

(Unit 16, #44)

Third Declension

Nom	**genus**	_____
Acc	_____	_____
Abl	_____	_____

(Unit 16, #55)

VI.

	First Declension		Second Declension (nom sg in -s)	
	sg	pl	sg	pl
Nominative	**sīmia**	_____	**lupus**	_____
Accusative	_____	_____	_____	_____
Ablative	_____	_____	_____	_____
Dative	_____	_____	_____	_____
Genitive	_____	_____	_____	_____
	(Unit 22, #159)	(Unit 23, #26)	(Unit 22, #161)	(Unit 23, #27)

	Second Declension (nom sg in Ø)		Second Declension Neuter	
	sg	pl	sg	pl
Nom	**vir**	_____	**rēgnum**	_____
Acc	_____	_____	_____	_____
Abl	_____	_____	_____	_____
Dat	_____	_____	_____	_____
Gen	_____	_____	_____	_____
	(Unit 22, #163)	(Unit 23, #28)	(Unit 22, #165)	(Unit 23, #29)

Third Declension (nom sg in -s)

	sg	pl
Nom	canis	
Acc		
Abl		
Dat		
Gen		
	(Unit 22, #167)	(Unit 23, #30)

Third Declension (nom sg in Ø)

	sg	pl
Nom	leō	
Acc		
Abl		
Dat		
Gen		
	(Unit 22, #169)	(Unit 23, #31)

Third Declension Neuter

	sg	pl
Nom	genus	
Acc		
Abl		
Dat		
Gen		
	(Unit 22, #171)	(Unit 23, #32)

Fourth Declension

	sg	pl
Nom	manus	
Acc		
Abl		
Dat		
Gen		
	(Unit 22, #173)	(Unit 23, #33)

Fifth Declension

	sg	pl
Nom	rēs	
Acc		
Abl		
Dat		
Gen		
	(Unit 22, #175)	(Unit 23, #34)

Fifth Declension

	sg	pl
Nom	diēs	
Acc		
Abl		
Dat		
Gen		
	(Unit 22, #177)	(Unit 23, #35)

QUESTION WORDS

I. INTERROGATIVE PRONOUNS

	Personal		Non-personal	
	sg	pl	sg	pl
Nom	**Quis?** _____	**Quī?** _____	**Quid?** _____	**Quae rēs?** _____
Acc	___ _____	_____	_____	_____
Abl	_____ (Unit 12, #465)	_____ (Unit 15, #185)	_____ (Unit 12, #465)	_____ (Unit 16, #366)
Dat	_____		_____	
Gen	_____ (Unit 22, #45)		_____ (Unit 22, #45)	

II.

	m & f	n
Nom	**Quālis?** _____	**Quāle?** _____
Acc	_____	_____
Abl	_____ (Unit 12, #468)	_____ (Unit 13, #154)

III.

	m	f	n
	uter (Unit 17, #245)	_____	_____

ADVERBS

īgn_____, **blan**_____, **avā**_____ (Unit 19, #110)

fort_____, **lev**_____, **sapie**_____ (Unit 19, #112)

PRONOUNS

I.

Singular

	m	f	n	
Nom	**hic**	**haec**	**hoc**	(Unit 17, #318)
Acc				
Abl				
Dat	**huic**	**huic**	**huic**	
Gen	**hujus**	**hujus**	**hujus**	

Plural

	m	f	n
Nom			
Acc			
Abl			
Dat	**hīs**	**hīs**	**hīs**
Gen	**hōrum**	**hārum**	**hōrum**

II.

Singular

	m	f	n	
Nom	**ille**	**illa**	**illud**	(Unit 17, #321)
Acc				
Abl				
Dat	**illī**	**illī**	**illī**	
Gen	**illīus**	**illīus**	**illīus**	

12

Plural

Nom	_____	_____	_____
Acc	_____	_____	_____
Abl	_____	_____	_____
Dat	**illīs**	**illīs**	**illīs**
Gen	**illōrum**	**illārum**	**illōrum**

III. PERSONAL PRONOUNS

	First Person		Second Person	
	sg	pl	sg	pl
Nom	**egō**	**nōs**	**tū**	**vōs**
Acc	_____	_____	_____	_____
Abl	_____	_____	_____	_____
Dat	_____	_____	_____	_____
Gen	_____	_____	_____	_____
	(Unit 26, #140)		(Unit 26, #143)	

The genitive singular of these pronouns is rarely found in Latin literature and not at all in *Latin: Level One.*

13

VERBS

I. #2 TENSE

First Conjugation

satiō _____ _____

_____ _____

_____

(Unit 25, #282)

Second Conjugation

placeō _____ _____

_____ _____

_____

(Unit 25, #283)

Third Conjugation (regular)

neglegō _____ _____

_____ _____

_____

(Unit 25, #284)

Third Conjugation (-iō)

sapiō _____ _____

_____ _____

_____

(Unit 25, #285)

Fourth Conjugation

custōdiō _____ _____

_____ _____

_____

(Unit 25, #286)

esse

sum _____ _____

_____ _____

_____

(Unit 25, #329)

posse

possum _____ _____

_____ _____

_____

(Unit 25, #350)

14

II. #1 TENSE

1st Conjugation

cēn_____ _____

_____ _____

_____ _____

(Unit 26, #36)

2d	3d
noc_____	**scrīb**_____
etc.	etc.
3d **-iō**	4th
cap_____	**aud**_____
etc.	etc.

(Unit 26, #37)

III. #3 TENSE

1st Conjugation

adjuvābō _____ _____

_____ _____

_____
(Unit 26, #220)

2d Conjugation

mordēbō _____ _____

_____ _____

_____
(Unit 26, #221)

3rd Conjugation

reddam _____ _____

_____ _____

_____
(Unit 26, #222)

3rd Conjugation (**-iō**)

aspiciam _____ _____

_____ _____

_____
(Unit 26, #223)

4th Conjugation

saliam _____ _____

_____ _____

_____
(Unit 26, #224)

IV.

esse

#1

eram _____ _____

_____ _____

_____
(Unit 26, #288)

#3

erō _____ _____

_____ _____

_____
(Unit 26, #290)

16

V.

#5 TENSE

fēcī _____ _____

_____ _____

_____

(Unit 27, #202)

#4 TENSE

fēceram _____ _____

_____ _____

_____

(Unit 28, #7)

#6 TENSE

fēcerō _____ _____

_____ _____

_____

(Unit 29, #40)

VI. VERB SYSTEM

	#1	#2	#3
Imperfective	_____	_____	_____
Perfective	#4 _____	#5 _____	#6 _____

(Unit 29, #39)

17

RELATIVE PRONOUNS

Singular

	m	f	n	
Nom	**quī**	**quae**	**quod**	(Unit 19, #322)
Acc				
Abl				
Dat	**cui**	**cui**	**cui**	
Gen	**cujus**	**cujus**	**cujus**	

Plural

	m	f	n	
Nom	**quī**	**quae**	**quae**	(Unit 28, #130)
Acc				
Abl				
Dat				
Gen				

SUMMARY OF QUESTION WORDS

I. INTERROGATIVE PRONOUNS

Singular

	m & f	n	
Nom	**Quis?**	**Quid?**	Expect as answer a noun in the same case and same environment. (See also #4 in Facts About Latin.)
Acc	**Quem?**	**Quid?**	
Abl	**Quō?**	**Quō?**	
Dat	**Cui?**	**Cui?**	
Gen	**Cujus?**	**Cujus?**	

Plural

	m	f	n
Nom	Quī?	Quae?	Quae?
Acc	Quōs?	Quās?	Quae?
Abl	Quibus?	Quibus?	Quibus?
Dat	Quibus?	Quibus?	Quibus?
Gen	Quōrum?	Quārum?	Quōrum?

For the nominative-accusative neuter plural (**Quae?**), the forms **Quae rēs?** and **Quās rēs?** are very common.

II. INTERROGATIVE ADJECTIVES

The general interrogative adjective **Quī?, Quae?, Quod?** has the forms of the relative pronoun.
Quālis?, Quāle? is answered by an adjective of quality.   (Units 12, 13, 17)
Quantus?, Quanta?, Quantum? is answered by an adjective of size.   (Units 13, 17)
Quotus?, Quota?, Quotum? is answered by an ordinal number.   (Unit 19)
Uter?, Utra?, Utrum? requires a choice between two answers.   (Unit 17)

III. OTHER WAYS TO ASK QUESTIONS

Quāliter? is answered by an adverb.   (Unit 19)
The enclitic **-ne,** attached to the first important word of the sentence, is answered in the following ways:

    if the answer is affirmative, by repetition of that word;
    if the answer is negative, by repetition of that word with a negator;
    if there is a choice (e.g. **Estne magister servus an līber?**), by
        repetition of one of the choices given.

An is used in a question to indicate an alternative between two answers.

PRINCIPAL PARTS OF VERBS

FIRST CONJUGATION

adjuvō	_____	_____	_____	(Unit 30, #22)
cantō	_____	_____	_____	(Unit 30, #25)
cūrō	_____	_____	_____	(Unit 30, #27)
indicō	_____	_____	_____	(Unit 28, #89)
laudō	_____	_____	_____	(Unit 30, #24)
lavō	_____	_____	_____	(Unit 30, #163)
mūtō	_____	_____	_____	(Unit 30, #26)
negō	_____	_____	_____	(Unit 30, #23)
stō	_____	_____		(Unit 28, #87)

cēnō	cēnāre	cēnāvī	
comparō	comparāre	comparāvī	comparātus
consummō	consummāre	consummāvī	consummātus
dō	dare	dedī	datus*
dōnō	dōnāre	dōnāvī	dōnātus
imperō	imperāre	imperāvī	imperātus
irrītō	irrītāre	irrītāvī	irrītātus
laxō	laxāre	laxāvī	laxātus
necō	necāre	necāvī	necātus
numerō	numerāre	numerāvī	numerātus
obumbrō	obumbrāre	obumbrāvī	obumbrātus
satiō	satiāre	satiāvī	satiātus
servō	servāre	servāvī	servātus
sīgnificō	sīgnificāre	sīgnificāvī	sīgnificātus

The principal parts of most First Conjugation verbs follow the pattern of sīgnificō, sīgnificāre, sīgnificāvī, sīgnificātus (-ō, -āre, -āvī, -ātus). This verb can therefore serve as a model for almost all other verbs of the First Conjugation. However, a few First Conjugation verbs do not follow this pattern. As you can see from the table above, these include adjuvō, adjuvāre, adjūvī, adjūtus; dō, dare, dedī, datus; lavō, lavāre, lāvī, lōtus; and stō, stāre, stetī.

---

*Dō, dare, dedī, datus is an irregular verb, but is often listed with the First Conjugation. However, the -a- is short in most of the forms.

SECOND CONJUGATION

dēbeō	_____	_____	_____	(Unit 28, #209)
fulgeō	_____	_____		(Unit 28, #95)
habeō	_____	_____	_____	(Unit 28, #91)
maneō	_____	_____		(Unit 28, #93)
palleō	_____	_____		(Unit 30, #29)
rīdeō	_____	_____	_____	(Unit 28, #197)
rubeō	_____	_____		(Unit 30, #31)
stupeō	_____	_____		(Unit 30, #30)
taceō	_____	_____		(Unit 28, #206)

moveō	**movēre**	**mōvī**	**mōtus**
noceō	**nocēre**	**nocuī**	
placeō	**placēre**	**placuī**	
possideō	**possidēre**	**possēdī**	**possessus**
teneō	**tenēre**	**tenuī**	
videō	**vidēre**	**vīdī**	**vīsus**

THIRD CONJUGATION

dīcō	_____	_____	_____	(Unit 30, #34)
metuō	_____	_____		(Unit 30, #35)
mittō	_____	_____	_____	(Unit 28, #203)
neglegō	_____	_____	_____	(Unit 28, #103)
pingō	_____	_____	_____	(Unit 30, #33)
pōnō	_____	_____	_____	(Unit 28, #97)
premō	_____	_____	_____	(Unit 30, #36)
quaerō	_____	_____	_____	(Unit 28, #99)
requīrō	_____	_____	_____	(Unit 30, #172)
tangō	_____	_____	_____	(Unit 28, #336)
trahō	_____	_____	_____	(Unit 28, #101)

āmittō	**āmittere**	**āmīsī**	**āmissus**
bibō	**bibere**	**bibī**	
cognōscō	**cognōscere**	**cognōvī**	**cognitus**
crēdō	**crēdere**	**crēdidī**	**crēditus**
currō	**currere**	**cucurrī**	
dīligō	**dīligere**	**dīlēxī**	**dīlēctus**
dūcō	**dūcere**	**dūxī**	**ductus**
edō	**edere**	**ēdī**	**ēsus**
emō	**emere**	**ēmī**	**ēmptus**
frangō	**frangere**	**frēgī**	**frāctus**
impōnō	**impōnere**	**imposuī**	**impositus**
lūdō	**lūdere**	**lūsī**	**lūsus**
nūbō	**nūbere**	**nūpsī**	**nūptus**
pāscō	**pāscere**	**pāvī**	**pāstus**
petō	**petere**	**petīvī**	**petītus**
rumpō	**rumpere**	**rūpī**	**ruptus**
tendō	**tendere**	**tetendī**	**tēnsus**
vincō	**vincere**	**vīcī**	**victus**

THIRD CONJUGATION (-iō)

aspiciō	_____	_____	_____	(Unit 28, #107)
capiō	_____	_____	_____	(Unit 28, #105)
fugiō	_____	_____		(Unit 28, #150)
incipiō	_____	_____	_____	(Unit 30, #39)
sapiō	_____	_____		(Unit 30, #38)

effugiō	effugere	effūgī	
ēripiō	ēripere	ēripuī	ēreptus
faciō	facere	fēcī	factus

FOURTH CONJUGATION

aperiō	_____	_____	_____	(Unit 28, #111)
custōdiō	_____	_____	_____	(Unit 30, #41)
inveniō	_____	_____	_____	(Unit 30, #42)
serviō	_____	_____	_____	(Unit 28, #109)

audiō	audīre	audīvī	audītus
saliō	salīre	saluī	
sentiō	sentīre	sēnsī	sēnsus

IRREGULAR VERBS

circueō	circuīre	circuī	
eō	īre	iī	
ferō	ferre	tulī	lātus
possum	posse	potuī	
subeō	subīre	subiī	
sum	esse	fuī	
volō	velle	voluī	

BASIC TEXT FOR *LATIN: LEVEL ONE*

I. BASIC SENTENCES

As each Basic Sentence appears in the text, write the Latin first and then the English equivalent.

Unit 2

1. **Vestis** _____

    Clothes _____

Unit 3

2. **Vēritātem** _____

    Time _____

3. **Hilarem** _____

    God _____

4. **M** _____

    O _____

Unit 4

5. **E** _____

    A _____

Unit 5

6. _____

    _____

7. _____

    _____

Unit 6

8. _____

_____

9. _____

_____

_____

10. _____

_____

_____

_____

Unit 7

11. _____

_____

_____

_____

12. _____

_____

_____

_____

Unit 8

13. _____

_____

_____

_____

25

14. _____

_____

_____

15. _____

_____

_____

_____

16. _____

_____

17. _____

_____

_____

18. _____

_____

Unit 9

19. _____

_____

Unit 10

20. _____

_____

21. _____

_____

_____

22. _____

_____

_____

Unit 11

23. _____

_____

24. _____

_____

_____

Unit 12

25. _____

_____

_____

26. _____

_____

27. _____

_____

28. _____

_____

29. _____

_____

Unit 13

30. _____

_____

27

31. _____

_____

32. _____

_____

_____

33. _____

_____

_____

_____

34. _____

_____

35. _____

_____

Unit 14

36. _____

_____

37. _____

_____

_____

38. _____

_____

39. _____

_____

_____

Unit 15

40. _____

_____

41. _____

_____

42. _____

_____

_____

43. _____

_____

44. _____

_____

Unit 16

45. _____

_____

_____

46. _____

_____

_____

47. _____

_____

48. _____

_____

_____

Unit 17

49. _____

_____

50. _____

_____

51. _____

_____

52. _____

_____

53. _____

_____

54. _____

_____

55. _____

_____

56. _____

_____

Unit 18

57. _____

_____

58. _____

_____

59. _____

_____

_____

60. _____

    _____

61. **Thāis** _____

    Quae _____

    _____

    _____

    _____

Unit 19

62. **Nōn** _____

    Bel _____

    _____

    _____

    _____

63. _____

    _____

    _____

64. _____

    _____

65. _____

    _____

    _____

66. _____

    _____

67. _____

_____

_____

68. _____

_____

_____

Unit 20

69. _____

_____

_____

70. _____

_____

_____

71. _____

_____

_____

_____

72. _____

_____

Unit 21

73. _____

_____

_____

74. _____

   _____

75. _____

   _____

   _____

   _____

76. _____

   _____

77. _____

   _____

   _____

78. _____

   _____

   _____

Unit 22

79. _____

   _____

   _____

80. _____

   _____

81. _____

   _____

82. _____

_____

_____

_____

83. _____

_____

84. _____

_____

_____

85. _____

_____

86. _____

_____

87. _____

_____

88. _____

_____

89. _____

_____

Unit 23

90. _____

_____

91. _____

_____

_____

92. _____

_____

_____

93. _____

_____

94. _____

_____

_____

_____

95. _____

_____

96. _____

_____

97. _____

_____

_____

_____

Unit 24

98. _____

_____

99. _____

_____

_____

_____

100. _____

_____

101. _____

_____

_____

_____

102. _____

_____

103. _____

_____

_____

_____

104. _____

_____

_____

Unit 25

105. _____

_____

_____

106. _____

_____

107. _____

_____

_____

_____

108. _____

_____

_____

_____

109. _____

_____

_____

110. _____

_____

_____

111. _____

_____

_____

_____

112. _____

_____

113. **Nōn** _____

_____

___ **Hoc** _____

_____

_____

_____

114. _____

_____

115. _____

_____

_____

_____

116. **Jam** _____

_____

lūn _____

_____

_____

_____

117. _____

_____

118. _____

_____

_____

119. _____

_____

120. _____

_____

121. _____

_____

_____

_____

122. _____

_____

123. _____

_____

Unit 27

124. **"Sic** _____

Ser _____

_____

_____

_____

125. _____

_____

_____

_____

126. **Nox** _____

int _____

_____

_____

_____

127. _____

_____

_____

_____

128. _____

_____

129. _____

_____

_____

_____

130. **Lūs** _____

tem _____

_____

_____

_____

131. _____

_____

132. _____

_____

133. _____

_____

_____

_____

134. _____

_____

_____

135. _____

_____

_____

136. _____

    _____

    _____

Unit 28

137. _____

    _____

138. **Nōn** _____

    _____

    Qua _____

    _____

    _____

    _____

Unit 29

139. _____

    _____

    _____

140. **Dōn** _____

    tem _____

    _____

    _____

    _____

141. **Cit** _____

    at _____

    _____

    _____

    _____

    _____

II. READINGS

Unit 28

1. **Sī** _____

    _____

    "For _____

Sī _____

    _____

    ēdi _____

When _____

    _____

    "Mar _____

    _____

If _____

    _____

    You _____

2. **Bel** _____

   et _____

   Sed _____

   nec _____

   You _____

   _____

   And _____

   But _____

   _____

   You _____

   _____

3. **Nūp** _____

   _____

   Quod _____

   Dia _____

   _____

   What _____

   _____

4. **Lan** _____

   _____

   vēn _____

43

Cen _____

_____

   Nōn _____

   _____

I _____

_____

_____

_____

A _____

_____

   I _____

   _____

Unit 29

5. **Lau** _____

_____

   mē _____

Ec _____

_____

   Hoc _____

_____

My _____

_____

   and _____

_____

Look! _____

_____

I _____

6. **Hos** _____

   Hocc _____

You _____

_____

You _____

_____

Unit 30

7. **Qu** _____

   sed _____

O _____

_____

But _____

_____

8. **Thā** _____

_____

   Ūn _____

45

Qu

_____

   Th

_____

9. **Eut**

   exp

  Wh

_____

   and

_____

10. **Frŭ**

   Nē

  In

_____

   No

_____

11. **Dif**

_____

   Nec

You _____

_____

_____

I _____

12. **Lōt** _____

_____

inv _____

Tam _____

_____

In _____

He _____

_____

and _____

_____

Fau _____

_____

In _____

_____

INDEX TO *LATIN: LEVEL ONE*

Latin Grammar & Resources

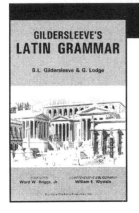

Gildersleeve's Latin Grammar
B.L. Gildersleeve & G. Lodge

The classic Latin grammar favored by many students and teachers with two new addtions:

✦ Foreword by **Ward W. Briggs, Jr.**
✦ Comprehensive bibliography by **William E. Wycislo.**

"Rightly interpreted, grammar is the culmination of philological study, and not its rudiment ... No study of literature can yield its highest result without the close study of language, and consequently the close study of grammar."

Basil L. Gildersleeve, *Selected Classical Papers*

"Compare his work with any other treatise hitherto in use, and its superiority will be manifest."

Southern Review

613 pp. (1895, third ed., reprint with additions 1997) paperback, ISBN 0-86516-353-7

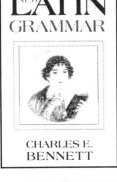

New Latin Grammar
Charles E. Bennett

New Latin Grammar uses specific examples from primary sources to help students learn the inflections, syntax, sounds, accents, particles and word formations of the Latin language. It also includes a history of the Indo-European family of languages, the stages of the development of the Latin language and sections on prosody, the Roman calendar, Roman names, and definition and examples of figures of syntax and rhetoric.

xvi + 287 pp. (1908, Reprint 1995) paperback, ISBN 0-86516-261-1

New Latin Syntax
E. C. Woodcock

This book gives a historical account of the chief Latin constructions, aiming to equip students to interpret texts as well as to write correct Latin. The index of passages quoted makes it useful as a reference work for teachers. This is a necessary reference and an indispensable vademecum for teachers and advanced students.

xxiv + 267 pp. (1959, Reprint 1987) Paperback, ISBN 0-86516-126-7

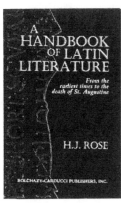

A Handbook of Latin Literature
From the earliest times to the death of St. Augustine
H. G. Rose

This reference work offers a matchless overview of Latin literature. Also included is a supplementary bibliography by E. Courtney.

582 pp. (1936, rpt. 1996), Paperback, ISBN: 0-86516-317-0

Graphic Latin Grammar
James P. Humphreys

Four double-sided pages containing all your Latin grammar charts on sturdy card stock ready for insertion in a 3-ring notebook.

(1961, Reprint 1998) Four 3-hole-punched laminated reference cards, ISBN 0-86516-460-6

Elementary Latin Translation: Latin Readings for Review
A. E. Hillard and C. G. Botting, eds., with additions by Donald H. Hoffman

This graded reader is an excellent supplement to first-year Latin texts or as a review tool. The Latin is pure, simple, idiomatic, and easily understood by beginning students. Each review features two readings that acquaint the student with the chief events of Roman history and stories from Greek mythology. Latin references eliminate the need to consult other grammars.

vii + 192 pp. (1961, Reprint 1997), Paperback, ISBN 0-86516-403-7

BOLCHAZY-CARDUCCI Publishers, Inc.
orders@bolchazy.com

Latin in Music
—Sine musica nulla disciplina potest esse perfecta; nihil enim est sine illa.—

Vergil's Dido and Mimus Magicus *New*
composed by Jan Novák, conducted by Rafael Kubelik

An oratorio of two famous Vergil passages: *Dido,* taken from the fourth book of the *Aeneid;* and *Mimus Magicus,* from Vergil's eighth *Eclogue* on **CD**. Includes a libretto in Latin, English, and German. New import to America. Originally recorded by *audite* Schallplatten, Ostfildern, Germany, 1986.

Limited Edition CD (1997), 40-page libretto in Latin, English and German, ISBN 0-86516-346-4

Schola Cantans *New*
composed by Jan Novák

A **cassette** and **dual language libretto** with musical arrangement of *Catullus* (34) Dianae Sumus in Fide; *Catullus* (5) Vivamus Mea Lesbia; *Catullus* (61) Collis O Heliconii; *Horace* (Carm. I.22) Integer Vitae; *Horace* (Carm. I.2) Iam Satis Terris; *Horace* (Epod. 15) Nox Erat; Gaudeamus Igitur; Nautarum Carmen; *Caesar* (BG I.1-3) Gallia Est Omnis Divisa; *Carmina Burana* (142) Tempus Adest Floridum; *Carmina Burana* (85) Veris Dulcis in Tempore; *Phaedrus* (I.13) Vulpis et Corvus; and *Martial* (62) Ludi Magister.

Cassette and Libretto: (1998) ISBN 0-86516-357-X; *Music Score:* (1998) ISBN 0-86516-358-8
Cassette, Libretto, and Music Score Set: (1998) ISBN 0-86516-404-5

Latin Music Through the Ages
Cynthia Kaldis

The illustrated book includes the Latin text, English translation, vocabulary, essays, and bibliography to accompany the musical performance. The seventeen Latin songs are directed by Clayton Lein and sung by the Lafayette Chamber Singers.

Songs include *The Virgin's Cradle Hymn* (Rubbra), *Mirabile Mysterium* (Handl), *Ave Regina Coelorum* (Dufay), *Ave Generosa* (Hildegard), *Ubi Caritas* (Duruflé) *Ave Verum* (Poulenc), *Non Nobis Domine* (Byrd), *O Sacrum Convivium* (Messaien), *Poculum Elevatum* (Arne), *O Vox Omnes* (Casals)

Book: Illus., xli + 87 pp. (1991) Paperback, ISBN 0-86516-242-5
Cassette: ISBN 0-86516-249-2

Latine Cantemus: Cantica Popularia Latine Reddita
Franz Schlosser, *trans. and illus.*

This illustrated edition features ✦ 60 new Latin translations ✦ traditional Latin favorites ✦ Christmas songs ✦ well-known Gregorian chants.

Illus., vii + 135 pp. (1996), Paperback, ISBN 0-86516-315-4

Carmina Burana
Judith Sebesta

Carl Orff's selections of twenty-four *"cantiones profanae"* from the Middle Ages are explored in this illustrated, dual-language edition featuring the original Latin poems with facing translations and vocabulary, complete vocabulary, bibliography, and study materials. Also included is a literary translation by Jeffrey M. Duban. In addition to medieval woodcutes, this new edition contains seventeen original illustrations by Thom Kapheim.

Illus. 165 pp. (Enhanced reprint 1996), Paperback, ISBN 0-86516-268-9

*M*usic hath charms to soothe the savage breast,
To soften rocks, or bend a knotted oak.
I've read that things inanimate have moved,
And, as with living souls, have been inform'd
By magic numbers and persuasive sound.
The Mourning Bride, Act I

**BOLCHAZY-CARDUCCI
Publishers, Inc.**
http://www.bolchazy.com